BRENCHLEY AND MATFIELD

REV

A PICTORIAL RE
HISTORY OF THE VILLAGES OF
BRENCHLEY AND MATFIELD IN KENT

THE BRENCHLEY AND MATFIELD
LOCAL HISTORY SOCIETY

Printed by Fleet Litho (Kent) Ltd

BRENCHLEY AND MATFIELD REVISITED

PUBLISHED BY

THE BRENCHLEY AND MATFIELD

LOCAL HISTORY SOCIETY

ISBN 978-0-9540936-2-4

This book is dedicated to

ROY CLAYDON

who, for twelve years from 1996 to 2008, was Secretary and Vice-Chairman to the Brenchley and Matfield Local History Society. He did an enormous amount of work towards the production of this book but, sadly, did not live to see its publication.

Throughout the book (with one exception on p.56) modern photographs are in colour and old photographs are in black and white.

William Hodges with all his badges of office: the horn to announce his presence; the baton, presumably to ward off marauding dogs, together with his top hat and satchel.

INTRODUCTION BY THE PRESIDENT MICHAEL GIBBONS

Brenchley and Matfield were extremely fortunate to have in the 1860s William Hodges as their letter carrier. His hobby, and it must have been more than just a hobby, was the relatively new field of photography. Assisted and succeeded by his son Frank they made an extensive record of the buildings in the villages as well as of many of the working inhabitants.

When the Hodges' glass plates were discovered in the 1970s they were given to the recently formed Brenchley and Matfield Local History Society, and lodged by them for safe keeping with the Kent County Archives Office at Maidstone. Considerable thought was given to the best use to which this remarkable collection should be put. A small selection of photographs was displayed in the Parish Room, the cost of framing being met by Portobello resident Barry Williams, but the obvious course was to publish in book form. A sub-committee was formed with the local Amenity Society and some effort put into sorting the photographs into meaningful groups. However it was only when my successor as chairman, Mrs Susan Edwards, took office that her enthusiasm and energy saw the task accomplished and 'A Victorian Pictorial Record of Brenchley and Matfield' was published to great and deserving acclaim.

Now, more than twenty five years later, the enthusiasm of the current committee under the leadership of Mrs Denise Barr has given us the opportunity to view many of these historic images again. This time though we have the contrast of contemporary photographs, most of them taken especially for this book, of the same subjects placed alongside the originals.

This juxtaposition of the late 19th century with the early 21st century will be of great interest to present residents and friends of the villages, and will as well provide a fascinating record for future students and historians.

In my view this is an admirable way for any local history society to fulfil its main objectives, and we can be proud of our own society for having, in the words of the maxim, "cherished the past, honoured the present and created for the future".

WILLIAM HODGES

William Hodges was born in 1820, the only son of Elizabeth and William Hodges, labourer, and was baptized in Brenchley on the 26th November. At the age of twenty four he married Elizabeth Diprose of Horsmonden, who was then aged eighteen. They had four children: Jonas, Mary, Frank and Jabez. On his marriage William's occupation was given as 'shoemaker' and Elizabeth's as 'dressmaker'. We know that in 1861 the Hodge Family was living at No.1 Laurel Cottages, Market Heath, and that William was employed as the local Rural Letter Carrier.

These were the very early days of photography and it became a lifelong hobby of William, although later it became more than a hobby. The Brenchley Local Directory of 1884 lists him as 'William Hodges – Photographer'. Portrait photography became popular where the subjects came to the studio and the equipment was kept in one place. What makes William's photography special is that he travelled many miles in order to photograph all aspects of village life. He carried all his cumbersome equipment with him, not only his bulky camera, several lenses and tripod, but also glass bottles of chemicals for coating, sensitizing, developing and fixing. He would need glass plates for the pictures, dishes, funnels, buckets for water and, of course, sometimes the water itself. He would also need a portable table and dark tent for the developing process. The Village Archive has many of Mr Hodges' bills, dating from 1842 to 1888, for the purchase of chemicals from Maidstone.

After William's death his son Frank continued taking photos. For many years their glass plates were lost, so it was an amazing find when, during repairs to the Hodges' house in the 1970s, some were found in an old laundry basket. Later others were found in the Parish Room, some being used as teapot stands! They are now safely stored in the County Archive in Maidstone and the Brenchley and Matfield Local History Society is fortunate in having the copyright.

When Walter Monckton of the Old Parsonage (now called Brenchley Manor) moved to Borough Green, the Parish presented him with a book of photographs of the local scenes as a memento and thanks for his help over many years in the village. These photographs would probably have been taken by William Hodges, and it is certainly possible and rather nice to conjecture that many of the wonderful photographs that William Hodges left us were taken for this gift.

William Hodges' home 'The Laurels', now known as 'Cornerways', at the corner of Petteridge Lane.

Above: William Hodges' wife visits the travelling library outside the toll cottage at the end of Petteridge Lane.

Below: One of Hodges' photographs of a locomotive at Tunbridge Wells Station.

Presented to

WILLIAM HODGES,

POSTMAN

IN MATFIELD DISTRICT, OF THE PARISH OF BRENCHLEY,

WITH THE

Sincere Regard of his Friends and Neighbours

in testimony of the faithful and courteous discharge of his duties

FOR 28 YEARS.

Ten Pounds accompanies this assurance of their esteem

MARKET'S HEATH, BRENCHLEY.

LADIES AND GENTLEMEN,

I beg most sincerely, to thank all of my friends and neighbours, for the kind *TESTIMONIAL* presented to me, and to state that I feel myself unworthy to receive from the Rev. F. Storr, and other kind friends in the district such an acknowledgement of past services.

I am Ladies and Gentlemen,

your obedient servant,

WILLIAM HODGES.

NOVEMBER 25 th, 1882.

THE SHAPING OF OUR PARISH

The oldest evidence we have of habitation in the area is the earth-work or 'castle' situated in Castle Hill. The exact date of the construction is unknown but it has been classified as a 'moat camp' and the moat still retains some water even though it is situated on a hill-side. The entrenchments are not in a good state of preservation and the site is very overgrown. However, the work appears to have consisted of a deep fosse, or moat, with ballast thrown on both sides to form two ramparts. There is evidence of a second ditch and a third rampart on two parts of the circle and the only opening is on the south-east, which is, presumably, the original entrance.

In early times the Weald was covered with oak forest; the woods less valued for their timber than for the acorns and 'dens' (wooded glades) where pigs could be kept. Later on, as the forest began to be cleared, the 'dens' became the settlements and villages (hence Wealden villages incorporating 'den' in their names - Horsmonden, Tenterden, Marden).

Brenchley must have originated as a clearing in the forest: this is what 'ley' means, from the Saxon, 'Braence's clearing'. In 1170 a chapel in Brenchley was part of the vast Parish of Eldyrige (Yalding) and belonged to the de Clare family. There is evidence structurally that some of the present church is Saxon. Richard de Clare granted the Parish to Tonbridge Priory, which he had recently founded, and from then on Brenchley is referred to as a separate parish. The present church, we are told, was built in 1233, in the 'Early English' period of church architecture. It is built of local sandstone, thought to have been quarried at Pixot Hill.

During the early 14th Century cloth-making, with its headquarters in Cranbrook, became established by clothiers and weavers from Flanders. Villages like Brenchley became involved in this flourishing trade and many of the substantial timber-framed buildings throughout the Weald were built with the wealth of this industry.

The Weald was also, in later years, a centre for the iron industry, and names in the parish refer to this: Furnace Pond, Furnace Farm, Cinderhill. Brenchley is not listed in the Elizabethan lists of Kent foundries and furnaces but, under James I, John Brown of Brenchley became prominent as an ironmaster. By 1613 he was well established, employing 200 men, and the following year he was granted the monopoly of making iron and brass guns for the navy. By 1642 he had become the gunfounder for Parliament. The Medway was used as an easy route to the Thames and London. Today it is hard to imagine the fiery furnaces of the iron industry belching smoke into the valleys of the Weald; the tranquil ponds are all we have left, although below Cinderhill Wood there are some masses of what is possibly spent moulding sand. With ship-building, the iron industry and clearing, the oaks of the Weald became fewer. We can see that the oak-studding in the earlier buildings is much closer than in the later ones.

In the late 18th Century, when Hasted, the Kent historian, made his way through the Weald, he found the roads "very deep and miry" and the parish as having a "dreary, gloomy aspect from the quantity of large spreading oaks throughout it". He goes on to say, "the houses, which are mostly old-fashioned timbered buildings, are situated in general round the different small greens or fostals". At this time the Parish of Brenchley included the hamlets of Matfield and Paddock Wood.

Clearly it was quite difficult to travel far and Brenchley, like many villages, was more or less self-sufficient. In 1823 The Directory lists people under the following trades: blacksmiths, bricklayers, butchers, carpenters, corn-millers, grocers and drapers, nursery and seedmen, plumbers and glaziers, saddlers, shoemakers, surgeons, tailors, taverners, beersellers and wheelwrights. Hatmill Cottage stands on the banks of a stream in Hatmill Lane and, as the name suggests, it was here that straw and beaver hats were made. Also, as its name suggests, Bramble Reed Lane, Matfield, was once a centre for the thatching industry. Marl (Marle Place) was dug for spreading on ground around lime-loving crops, as agriculture, of course, was a mainstay of the area, with hops and fruit predominating at this time. There was employment locally on the farms, in the local shops and with the local tradesmen, as well as domestic work in the big houses.

The repair of the main road from London to Goudhurst, from 1750, was carried out by a Turnpike Trust, and there were toll gates at Burrs Hill, Market Heath, Cork's Pond (where Matfield War Memorial now stands) and Brenchley Hill (Paygate Cottage). In 1823 passengers could travel by coach to London on Mondays, Wednesdays and Fridays, returning on Tuesdays, Thursdays and Saturdays, aboard the 'Flower of Kent'. The stage-coach service was eclipsed with great speed by the advent of rail travel and Paddock Wood station opened in 1842.

The coming of the railway brought enormous changes; people could travel further afield to work and a rapid expansion of the villages followed. The population of Kent trebled in the 19th Century. Both Matfield and Paddock Wood, originally part of the Ecclesiastical Parish of Brenchley, now became Parishes in their own right, and St. Luke's Church was built in 1876. Today few residents of Matfield and Brenchley work within the villages. Most of the population is either retired or travels to work elsewhere - hence the predominance now of the motor car. The quiet country lanes we see in William Hodges' photographs have gone forever and our roads seem to be getting busier every year.

ALL SAINTS' CHURCH, BRENCHLEY

In Mediaeval times the Parish was owned in part by Bertram de Criol, Sheriff of Kent in the time of Henry III (1250); the name lingers on as Cryals. The chapel was rebuilt as a church in 1170, though not completed until 1233, using stone quarried below Pixot Hill.

The substantial base walls of the tower, in places ten feet thick, were necessary to support the steeple, one of the tallest in the county, being over 200 feet high. This stood until 1703, when a great storm destroyed it, to the delight of the children who were able to claim that they had jumped over the church steeple.

A booklet with a full history of this Grade I listed building is for sale in the Church.

A photograph by William Hodges of a sketch of Brenchley Church showing windows in the main roof.

Views of All Saints' Church from the South.

BRENCHLEY CHURCH BELLS

There are eight bells. Until 1924 the ring was six; of these the present numbers 3, 4 and 6 were made by the Whitechapel Foundry, dated respectively 1836, 1720 and 1813. The other three, the present 5, 7 and 8, were founded by Joseph Hatch of Ulcombe and Broomfield (who also cast the Great Harry Bell in Canterbury Cathedral) and are all dated 1610. Number 8 weighs 18cwt (914.5 Kilos).

In 1924 numbers 1 (treble) and 2 were added, being the gift of Captain Lees of 'The Knowle' and Captain J. Ruxton of 'The Crooke'. The original six bells were then brought into line by tuning. This is probably the date of the photograph above.

The bells are inscribed with their dates and foundries. Number 4 (1720) is also inscribed "Intactum sileo percute dulce cano" (roughly translated: "Untouched I am a silent thing but strike me and I sweetly sing"). Two of the 1610 bells (numbers 5 and 8) are inscribed with Churchwardens' names: 'Thomas Fyshenden' and 'William Hunt'. The 1813 bell (number 6) is inscribed 'John Relph and I. Wimshurst Churchwardens'.

BRENCHLEY FROM THE TC

The upper photograph was taken by William Hodges from the Brenchley Church tower. Note the warehouses at the entrance to the church, where the lych-gate is now, and the cottages to the right of the yew trees within the churchyard. 'South Cottage' does not yet have the dormer windows in the roof. The lower photograph, taken by Mike Daniels recently, shows the centre of the village as it is now but still much the same as it was in the middle of the last century.

F THE CHURCH TOWER

Above: A drawing of the new lychgate, which replaced the warehouse and cottages.
Below: One of the warehouses and the corner of one of the cottages can just be seen to the left. The cottages were considered to be unhygienic and needed to be demolished. A sum of £400 was to be raised in this connection.

BRENCHLEY VILLAGE

Above: The photograph shows the village before the 'Bull Inn' burned down. This aspect of the 'Old Palace', seen on the right, shows the roof before the gables were added. A story is told that a travelling tinker stopped at the old 'Bull Inn'. He set his gluepot to heat on the stove whilst lingering over a pint at the bar. The pot boiled over and set alight, causing the destruction of the earlier building. The new 'Bull Inn' was built in 1888.

Below: Brenchley High Street, showing the 'Old Post Office' on the right, demolished in 1965 to widen the road.

Above: The photograph is not one of William Hodges' but it shows the relaxed nature of the village street. This picture was taken after the restoration of the Old Palace in the 1880s and one of the new gables can be seen at the far end. As well as the cattle returning to pasture after milking, there is a horse drawn milk float and a boy on a bicycle outside the Old Palace. Barsley's department store in Paddock Wood was started in 'The Old Palace'.
Below: A present day view.

The newly rebuilt 'Bull Inn', Brenchley. In 1884 Mr. John Stapley was the proprietor. The wagonette brake was used for carrying passengers or exercising carriage horses.

THE BULL INN, BRENCHLEY

William Hodges' earlier photograph of the centre of Brenchley village shows the original old timber-framed Bull Inn, which was destroyed by fire. Hodges' later photograph opposite, taken in the 1880s, shows the newly built Bull, which has changed very little since then. We can see that "good stables and coach house" was advertised.

This High Victorian building is very different from the other pre-1700 tile-hung and timber-framed buildings in the centre of the village, but this can be seen as an interesting foil.

The barn to the rear of the building, like so many outbuildings today, has recently been converted to residential use.

These are just two of William Hodges' photographs showing some of the varied subjects that he liked to portray. We do not know who the people in these pictures were, nor where the photographs were taken, but they really capture the spirit of the time.

Above: A woman with a besom broom

Right: Four men and a dog, after a shoot

TERRY'S

THE BUTCHER'S SHOP AND TOWN FARM, BRENCHLEY

This very interesting framed building of high status was probably built around the late 1400s. It is thought that originally its function was non-domestic and might have been for some sort of public use. There is no evidence of central fires as there is no soot blackening in the roof. There is a story that it was used as a hunting lodge by Queen Anne, but there is no evidence to support this.

It was certainly used as a farm house for a great portion of its life, and some of the outbuildings that went with the farm can be seen in the photographs. Some have now been demolished but the oast house is still very much part of the centre of Brenchley.

The butcher's shop was certainly in existence in William Hodges' time. It is currently run by Terry Tester and his son, Neil, who can be seen standing in front of the shop in the modern picture. Terry worked in the shop for Mr. Wade for a number of years and, after he died, with his daughter Julie until she retired in 1980, when Terry took over the business. Neil joined his father when he left school.

The children appear to be waiting for something in front of the butcher's shop in Brenchley. Anyone would be a little foolhardy to be standing there nowadays as the traffic does rather sweep around the corner from Church Hill.

Above: Town Farm Oast in 1940 before renovation.
Below: Town Farm Oast in 1982 while renovations were underway.

Above: Town Farm situated behind the Brenchley butchery, where some of the buildings were once used as an abbatoir.
Below: Town Farm Barn, now the gardens of 1-4 Church Close.

Above: Enough of South Cottage is shown to see that the early photograph was taken before the addition of dormer windows. Below: Church House at the present time.

CHURCH HOUSE AND SOUTH COTTAGE

Church House was originally built in the early to mid 1600s. During the early 18th Century classical architecture became fashionable and many older buildings were re-fronted in the classical symmetrical design, including Church House. These façades were often built to hide the lower part of the old roof supposedly to "improve" proportions. The façade of Church House is rather special as it was done with weather-boarding but this was chamfered and grooved in imitation of rusticated stone. It is interesting that although alterations like this would never be allowed today, because it was done three hundred years, or so, ago it must be preserved!

A small oak was planted in 1863 to commemorate the marriage between the Prince of Wales (later Edward VII) and Princess Alexandra. This tree died and our present tree was planted as a replacement two years later. The small drinking fountain by the tree was erected to commemorate the Coronation of George V in 1911.

Mrs Rebekah Peacey, now 101, our oldest resident, lives in South Cottage with her daughter Mary.

Above: An Aveling & Porter 8 horse power traction engine built around 1888, delivering coal from Paddock Wood to Brenchley. Below: An Aveling and Porter 8 horse power traction engine built in 1874 and later converted to a road roller. Both were owned by William Lambert of Horsmonden who is thought to be seated at front of the rear roller.

A modern view of the Old Palace from the west side.

THE OLD PALACE

This grand timber-framed building was built around the middle of the 1400s and was clearly a building of some importance. Historically it was connected with the Moatlands Estate, which belonged to the Pimpe family. After the death of Reginald Pimpe in the reign of Henry VII it came into the possession of Thomas Roberts, mercer, remaining in the Roberts family until 1958. The worn brass memorials to Thomas and his three wives can be found in the Church.

Legend has it that the Duke of St. Albans, eldest son of Charles II and his mistress Nell Gwyn, was sent off to live in the country and took up residence in the Roberts great house in Brenchley. The house then became known as the 'Duke of St. Albans' Palace', or now, just 'The Old Palace'.

Originally what we see from the road would have been the rear of the building and the front would have been approached down the hill.. The gables, which seem so naturally part of the building, were added during restoration work in the 1880s. Apparently new beams for this work were brought from Glassenbury on wagons drawn by a pair of oxen. William Hodges took several pictures of the Old Palace at this time and would have seen this restoration work take place.

In 1943 the village Post Office and Stores moved into the 'Old Palace', which by now was divided up into several dwellings with an average rent of 7s. 6d (37p) per week. The 'Old Cottage' from which the Post Office used to operate and which stood on the site of 'The House' opposite 'Portobello' was demolished in 1965 in order that the road could be widened and straightened.

By 1958 the 'Old Palace' and the 'Old Workhouse' were both in a terrible state of disrepair and the expected restoration cost was so high that it was impossible to find a private purchaser. In order to avoid the demolition of two such historically and aesthetically important buildings Tonbridge Rural Council bought them both for the ridiculously low price of £4,200. Work began in 1962 and was completed by 1965 and restoration had cost £30,000, a huge price at that time. As well as dwelling houses, the 'Old Palace' retained the Post Office and the Parish Room.

Recently, once again, there has been great disquiet in the Parish regarding the structural state of these two buildings, and it has meant the loss of several Housing Association owned houses in the village as they have once again returned to private ownership. It is wonderful to see these two magnificent buildings restored to such a high standard and their future once again secure.

THE OLD VICARAGE AND SHOP, BRENCHLEY

This former vicarage is an extremely interesting and unspoilt traditional house, originally built in the 16th century with various phases of extensions and refurbishment, including a fine late seventeenth century parlour. The parlour is remarkable in having its original scheme of painted decoration almost intact. The overmantle is decorated with three 17th century landscape paintings. The Crown-post roof has 19th century graffiti, which includes interesting comments on local people. The adjoining building was a 19th century shop and still has its mahogany-topped counter complete with spice drawers. William Hodges' photograph shows the draper's shop trading under the name of 'Guest'. The archive has several bills and advertisements dating from this time.

THE ROSE & CROWN INN AND 'BOURNES'

This range of buildings was built in the 17th Century and probably formed part of the outbuildings of 'The Old Palace'. The 'Rose and Crown', which served the village for over 300 years, was recently sold to a developer who converted it to three houses and built a new house on the car park.

Mike and Caroline Kehoe retired in 2003 after running 'Bourne Store' for twenty five years. Since then, for very short periods, it has been an organic grocers, a gallery and a gift shop. At present the shop is vacant.

Below: Mr Bourne with his family and staff around 1910.

Mike Kehoe in September 2003, just before his retirement, and the interior of his store.

Above: The Junior School with three teachers in William Hodges' time.
Below: The boys with their gardening tools in 1922.
Both photographs were taken outside their school.
Right: The old school house has been converted to residential use and can be found next door to the present school.

SCHOOLING IN BRENCHLEY AND MATFIELD

In the mid-18th century education for the poor was more or less non-existent, and the children had to work to help support their family. Prosperous families sent their children to private schools or educated them at home.

In 1763 John Porter gave a Trust Fund of £3 per year for the education of the poor people of Brenchley Parish. Thomas Everest, paid by Brenchley Workhouse, started a small school for boys. Some of the boys from the Workhouse were boarded out to local shopkeepers, blacksmiths, shoemakers etc. to learn a trade.

It wasn't until the 19th century that the State recognised its responsibilities in education. In 1841 a National School was planned in Brenchley. Mr. Courthorpe, a landowner, gave half an acre of land from Parsonage Farm, and the school, initially for boys only, cost £ 541 9 shillings to build.

A private school run by Charlotte Birt and Thomas Diamond was running at this time as well, and Parish Registers of this time show that while many men could write their names, this was not so common amongst their brides.

Francis Storr, the Vicar of Brenchley, who was very interested in education, started a small boys' school in his Vicarage in 1861. Other small, private schools were set up. There was one at Pimms in Matfield and the Misses Betts opened a ladies' boarding school at 'Little Portobello' on Windmill Hill. This school continued very successfully for fifty eight years with an excellent reputation, having up to ten pupils. The cost was £4 a term with £2 extra for drawing and music. In the beginning the National School at Market Heath had just thirty four pupils.

Charles Storr, the son of Francis, who was the first Vicar of Matfield, opened a boys' preparatory school, Matfield Grange School, in Sophurst Lane. This school ran successfully until the boys were evacuated during the second World War. The empty school was bombed and was never re-opened.

Today we can see the popularity of our school in Market Heath by the traffic chaos in the village at dropping off and picking up times!

The present Primary School

BRENCHLEY MANOR

The Renaissance gateway at Brenchley Manor, an architectural gem, is thought to be one of the earliest examples of Italian craftsmanship in England. The gateway is attributed to the Florentine sculptor Pietro Torrigiano, who had the distinction of being forced to flee his native city after breaking the nose of a colleague in a brawl. His injured victim was none other than Michaelangelo.

Close to the arch and next to the house stands another little known local wonder, the gigantic Domesday oak believed to have been grown from an acorn planted in the reign of Alfred the Great (871-899). Whether this magnificent tree is indeed more than a thousand years old may be open to question, but its massive dimensions are not. With a girth of more than thirty six feet it has clearly been lucky to escape the fate of other ancient oaks.

Built around 1522, during the reign of Henry VIII, the house is steeped in history. Originally a Tudor Hall House, it belonged to the Priory of Tonbridge when it was called the 'Old Rectory'. It later became known as the 'Old Parsonage' and only much later became known (incorrectly) as 'Brenchley Manor'. After the dissolution of the monasteries Cardinal Wolsey intended to use the estate to endow the great college he was founding at Oxford. However on Wolsey's fall from grace instead of remaining part of Christ Church (as Cardinal College became), it was forfeited to Henry VIII who later granted it to Paul Sydnor, the King's agent to the Spanish Court. In 1563 it passed into the hands of William Waller of Groombridge whose family sold the house to the Courthopes and three members of this family were vicars of Brenchley from 1744 until 1845.

In 1912 the 'Old Parsonage' passed out of the Courthope family and was bought by Mr C H Allfrey and then passed through several different hands before being acquired by its present owners May Beth and Barry Bruckmann.

Over the years the house has evolved from its original rectangular Tudor Hall House shape with the addition of two substantial wings and now forms a harmonious square. It has many beautiful rooms, perhaps the most striking of which is the Parlour with its exquisite linen fold panelling. In 1571 the house became the dower house of Dame Elizabeth Fane after the death of her first husband William Waller. It was she who was responsible for the panelling, which bears her coat of arms with the letters EF over the fireplace alongside those of her second husband George Fane. The panelling which was completed in 1573 is quite outstanding in its design and intricacy and can be compared with the linen fold panelling in the church which forms the lower part of a vanished rood screen. So prized was the linen fold panelling in the Parlour that it was apparently dismantled during the Second World War and stored in the church for safety. Elizabeth Fane died in 1593 but her memory lives on in All Saints' Church. On the wall on the right side of the altar can be found a memorial praising her goodness and generosity.

There are close connections between the house and the church not only because the house was home to three of Brenchley's vicars and one curate. There is even reputed to be a secret tunnel that links the church to the house although what purpose this would have served is less clear.

'Brenchley Manor', showing the 'Domesday Oak' to the right of the house.

Above: 'Broad Oak' can just be seen but it was demolished in the 1930s.
Below: The present entrance to Broad Oak.

BROAD OAK

The photograph shows a wedding group at the gates of 'Broad Oak'. Note the constable on duty.

It is 151 years since the formation of the Kent County Constabulary. In 1857 local communities, which formerly had been fairly isolated with people tending to live and die in the place in which they had been born, were being brought closer together by the new railways. Often there was a village constable responsible for law and order, but he was not answerable to any central authority: he interpreted the law according to the whims of the local squire, who was usually the local magistrate. This system resulted in varying penalties in different parishes.

When the Kent County Constabulary was formed in 1857 there were 222 officers and men under the command of a former soldier, Captain John Henry Hay Ruxton. The Ruxton's family home was 'Broad Oak', Brenchley, bought from John Hooker in 1785. The nerve centre for the new County Constabulary was a large house, 'Wren's Cross', in Maidstone. There was an acre of ground which accommodated the main administration and criminal investigation offices, barracks, training school, tailor's shop, stores and stables. There were also three houses: one for the 'lock-up keeper', a parade ground and paddock for horses.

Captain John Henry Hay Ruxton

In 1857 a constable did not have to read or write and in the early years there was no instruction period. Practically any hefty, healthy young man of known honesty was accepted, put into a uniform and began work the next day. He possibly received some instruction from another constable, and had occasional drill parades. The men also learnt jujitsu.

There was discipline from the start, for Ruxton's men came from many backgrounds: labourers, soldiers, sailors, clerks, ex-officers and mechanics. After three months they seem to have evolved into a fit and happy team of officers, with a feeling of comradeship. We are told in the 'Centenary Book' that it is a remarkable tribute to Ruxton's foresight that the basic pattern he fashioned remained unchanged during a hundred years of extraordinary development. After 37 years of service, in 1894, Captain Ruxton retired on £400 p.a.. At this time he had outserved every member of the force, for all the original 222 had either died, retired or left for other appointments.

The house shown in William Hodges' photograph was built in the 1700s. The earlier (probably mediaeval) Manor House of 'Broad Oak' was demolished to build it. In the 1930s the house was owned by a brewer, Mr.Simpson. He demolished the house and sold the land for building several houses. He could probably be said to be Brenchley's first 'developer'!

Above: Broad Oak before the alterations were carried out.
Below: Broad Oak after alterations carried out in 1860..
Opposite: Captain Ruxton planting a commemorative tree to celebrate the wedding of Edward, Prince of Wales to Princess Alexandra of Denmark, in March 1863.

Brenchley

PORTOBELLO

This handsome house was built in 1739 and named in celebration of Admiral Vernon's capture of Portobello during that year.

The house was built for Timothy Monckton the first Monckton surgeon of Brenchley and was remodelled and extended in 1839 for Jonathan Monckton. Jonathan is possibly the balding man to the right of the bride in the photograph. The wedding is probably that of Jonathan's daughter, Emma, to Dr Samuel Dyer in 1853. Jonathan was suddenly taken ill, and died six weeks after the wedding. There are several graves of members of the Monckton family to the east of the church. Lord Monckton of Brenchley who was President of the Brenchley and Matfield Local History Society was buried there in 2007.

The War Memorial, erected in 1920, now stands on the triangular piece of grass in front of the house. It is said that the village 'lock-up', known as 'the cage' because of its wooden barred construction., once stood on this site. It housed offenders until they could be taken to Maidstone gaol. The village stocks are also reputed to have been sited here.

Wedding group at Portobello House.

Above: Unveiling Brenchley War Memorial.
Below: A modern view of the Brenchley War Memorial.
The Women's Institute Scrapbook in the Local History Society archives has an entry to say that a Mr May remembers the pile of stones on the triangle, now occupied by the war memorial. People who wanted to stay the night at the Workhouse had to break up the stones to pay for their night's lodgings.

THE WORKHOUSE

Brenchley's workhouse is a particularly fine building and was built in the late 16th century by the Roberts family as a farmhouse for a yeoman farmer and became a workhouse in the early eighteenth century.

Workhouses were places where those unable to support themselves could go to live and work. The Poor Law of 1601 in the reign of Elizabeth I made no mention of workhouses but it did propose the building of housing for the elderly and chronically sick. Most poor relief at that time took the form of 'outdoor relief': grants of money clothing, food and fuel to those living in their own homes. However in the 17th century the workhouse system began to evolve as a way for parishes to decrease the amount of money that ratepayers had to pay. This form of 'indoor relief' was designed to deter the able-bodied who were required to work usually without pay.

Under the terms of a lease dated December 1732 Sir Walter Roberts leased his farmhouse in Brenchley to the Vicar and Churchwardens of All Saints', Brenchley, for the princely sum of £3 per annum. It was to remain a workhouse until 1835.

People ended up in the workhouse for many different reasons. Often it was because they were too poor, old or too ill to support themselves. This may have been due to a number of different factors including lack of work during periods of high unemployment, or having no family willing or able to provide care for them when they became elderly or sick. Pregnant women who were unmarried were very often disowned by their

Distant view of All Saints' Church Brenchley with Portobello on the left and the Old Workhouse on the right.

families and the workhouse was the only place they could go to give birth and bring up their children. The mentally ill were often also consigned to the workhouse.

A parliamentary report of 1777 recorded parish workhouses in operation in Tonbridge (for up to 130 inmates), Brenchley (up to 60), Horsmonden (20), Bidborough (6) and Hadlow (16). Life inside the workhouse was probably much like being in a small self-contained institution. Apart from the dormitories and a dining hall for eating we may expect Brenchley's workhouse to have had workrooms on the ground floor including probably a bakery and laundry and vegetable gardens and orchards outside.

The main constituent of the workhouse diet was bread. At breakfast this was supplemented by gruel or porridge. Workhouse broth, meat and potatoes and suet puddings were other items found on workhouse menus. Inmates, apart from the old and infirm, were expected to work and this would have entailed agricultural labour, wood chopping, stone breaking, corn grinding and oakum picking.

Everything changed when the Poor Law Amendment Act was passed in 1834. Prior to that the general philosophy was that the poor were essentially the victims of their own situation and to help them was a Christian duty. The thinking behind the 1834 Act was very different. The poor were seen as largely responsible for their own predicament and could change if they chose to do so. Poverty was believed to be largely the result of fecklessness, immorality, idleness and drunkenness and it was thought that too liberal a welfare regime would encourage these vices and discourage self-improvement and honest labour.

The 1834 Act swept away parish workhouses and in their place created a number of much larger Poor Law Unions with a centralised and more standardised structure. Inmates at Brenchley were moved to a new Union workhouse at Sandhill near Pembury which accommodated up to 500. An 1881 census of the inmates of the new Union workhouse reveals that 23 came from Brenchley. The youngest being Frederick Richard Hooper aged 3 and listed as a pauper, the oldest William Golding aged 80 an agricultural labourer.

Brenchley's workhouse since 1834 has been put to a number of different uses - as a meeting place for a men's coffee club, a lending library and most recently as social housing. It is now being transformed again into three distinctive self-contained houses.

Conditions varied from workhouse to workhouse but they were never prisons and it was generally a voluntary decision to enter them. Inmates were free to leave them if they wished. Some people known as

the "ins and outs" entered and left quite frequently treating the workhouse rather like a guest house, although others could expect to remain for the rest of their lives.

Above: The 'Old Workhouse'.
Below: A recent photograph.

Above: A phaeton standing outside part of the Hat Mill.
Below: The view we see today.

HATMILL

Hatmill Cottage stands on the banks of a stream in Hatmill Lane, as the name suggests, where a thriving industry of straw and beaver hats was carried out. They were so well made that they often passed from father to son. Rabbits, hares, musquash and beaver all gave their skins to make the very best quality hats.

The stream which flows out of the mill-pond at 'Owthorpe' used to drive the water-wheel, then it ran into pools or tanks. It then ran on to Cowden Farm where it turned another waterwheel and thence into the Furnace Pond and out of the parish. A stream rising at the back of 'Kingsmead', Matfield fed firstly the large pond at Petteridge. This pond is fairly recent and may have been constructed as a fish pond. There is certainly no evidence of any industrial machinery there and no records can be found to say that they ever existed. The stream runs on from there and is joined by the stream rising near the Matfield Post Office. Just beyond the point where those two streams met a mill pond was constructed beside Petteridge Lane, to the south of the footpath to 'Bombazine Cottage'. This pond is shown on the maps of the late eighteenth century but had gone by 1845. The stream then runs under the road and between here and Fairmans Lane fed two water-mills. From those it continued to supply Cowden Mill and the Furnace Pond on its way to the River Teise.

An Indenture, now in the County Archives, dated 21st December 1753 must be referring to the three Mills from Petteridge Lane, what was later to become the Hat Mill. The indenture is between John Nutley of Brenchley, Miller, and Solomon Norris, Yeoman (John Nutley seems to be leasing from Solomon Norris), "all that messuage or tenement called or known by the name of the Malthouse and two water-mills, formerly three water-mills". The indenture includes other property "late in the tenure of John Woodgate and now the said John Nutley".

What is now Hatmill Lane runs to the south of those mills towards Cryals. Field names shown in this tithe apportionment shows that two mills were still operating on this site in 1845 although one has been changed from a Corn Mill to the Hat Mill. We also learn that at this time Thomas Manwaring occupied the Mill. A Mr. Bulldock, who made hats, lived in a house in the High Street, Brenchley in the reign of Queen Elizabeth I.

'Wat Tyler's Cottage', Crooke Road.

WAT TYLER'S COTTAGE

This house, on the edge of Brenchley Village and overlooking the Medway Valley, is a very complete example of a late mediaeval open hall house.

There is a fable that Wat Tyler of the 'Peasants' Revolt' in 1351 lived in a cottage near the Crook, but there is no real evidence that this was the Wat Tyler of history. William McGonagall, the Victorian poet (reputedly the world's worst poet!), wrote a poem called 'Grif of the Bloody Hand' in which Wat Tyler rescued, and married, Violet Evesham of Brenchley, after she was snatched by Grif. It's not clear where William McGonagall got this story, but possibly from 'The Life and Adventures of Wat Tyler the Good and the Brave' published in 1851. Well – it's a nice story!

The large house known as 'The Crooke', which was next door to 'Wat Tyler's', was sold in 1966 but demolished, as it spoilt the view from 'Wat Tyler's'.

William Hodges' picture shows the large vegetable plot to the front of the house. This was common practice at this time.

'Crooke Oast' damaged by the hurricane in 1987.

'Gate House Farm ', old and recent.

GATE HOUSE

The group of buildings to the south of Brenchley village, known as Gate House Farm, is probably typical of many old farms throughout Kent. We see the old farmhouse, originally a yeoman's house dating from the 16th century, surrounded by old cottages and various farm buildings, constructed at intervals over the years as the farming industry waxed and waned, and moved from one type of farming to another. There are stables and barns and a twin oast from the days when hop growing was a major industry. There's a huge apple store and a large pond near by, dug to provide water for the farm.

The name 'Gate House Farm' comes from the toll gate which once stood on the Brenchley to Horsmonden road, and the Toll House can still be seen on the corner.

In more recent years, the barns, stables and oasts have all been converted into homes, so there is now a small community of families living on the farm. Dan and Anne Colman now live in the main farmhouse and the surrounding fields are let to a tenant farmer for sheep. Emrys Davies with his wife Di, who works at the Brenchley Surgery, live in a cottage on the farm. Emrys runs a sign-writing business from the old apple store. The pond has been dredged and is a sanctuary, not only for all sorts of wild life, but also for the fishermen from the Beech Tree Angling and Wildlife Preservation Society, who have bought the pond and can now escape from the stresses and strains of modern life with their fishing rods!

Above: This photograph is not one of William Hodges'. It was taken in 1900 and shows the residents of 'Gate House Farm'. Below: A photograph taken in 2002 of the residents from the same viewpoint.

Above: 'Gate House Farm' buildings.

Below: 'Paygate Cottage', the original toll house for herders and others to pay towards the upkeep of the road between Brenchley and Horsmonden. There would have been a gate across the road at this point to deter those attempting to scuttle through without paying. 'Gate House Farm' gets its name from this gate.

Looking South down Windmill Hill, Brenchley. Both 'Hill House' and 'Little Portobello' were once owned by the Monckton family.

WINDMILL HILL, BRENCHLEY

Hill House, previously called 'The Cottage', had a rear wing and front bay windows added in about 1880. Little Portobello, on the right, was once the home of Jonathan Monckton (see wedding group on page 35). It was later used as a school for young ladies. There seem to be no photographs of the former windmill at the top of Windmill Hill. The nearest we have seems to be the drawing shown below.

Above: This view of Brenchley is reproduced from a twentieth century postcard showing Brenchley from 'The Firs' in 1834, which was in the possession of T. Else. On the back of the card is an inscription signed by Eddy Lambert (founder of Lambert & Foster) that says: "Brenchley drawn from the front of The Firs (now Tawsden Manor in Spout Lane) showing the former windmill. I have played under the 5 Lombardy poplars in Peter's field." The figures in the foreground are probably Professor Hooker, founder of Kew Gardens, and his wife.

'Primrose Hill', Hill Top

PRIMROSE HILL

Primrose Hill was built on the site of the demolished windmill at the top of the hill in Brenchley. The buildings to the right of William Hodges' photograph would be the roof of the 'Windmill Tavern'.

The house was named after the lease dating from 1569, in which rent of one primrose was to be paid on Easter Day. Several properties were subject to this 'Primrose Rent', but it was lost in the mists of time to whom it should be paid.

The photograph below shows a gathering outside the 'Windmill Tavern' in the early 1880's. This public house was situated at the top of Windmill Hill, on the site of 'Windmill Cottage' which was built when the pub was demolished. At this time the pub was run by Henry Adolphus Watkins (born 1838, and known as Adolphus) and his wife Elizabeth (born 1842). They lived there with their children.

Henry and Elizabeth were married in 1860 and the 1871 census tells us that he was living at the 'Walnut Tree' and working as a milkman. The 1881 census shows Henry living at 'Windmill Tavern' as a beerhouse keeper.

THE TOLL GATE, MARKET HEATH

Above: William Hodges' photograph shows his wife and child standing by the toll house, which stood on the Brenchley Road near to the turning to Petteridge. Below: A photograph from the same viewpoint today.

Above: A drawing of Mrs Dickinson and her dog 'Frisk' at the Toll Gate, Market Heath in about 1849.
Below: A delivery cart at the Toll Gate.

MARKET HEATH

'Wisteria Cottages', Market Heath, showing very little change over the years.

Above: Early threshing machine outside 'Wisteria Cottages', pulled by a six horse power Aveling and Porter traction engine, built 1871. Note the wooden wheels and a man in front with a warning flag. This machine was owned by George Ellis who had a farm near 'Blue Boys'.
Below: The lower picture shows a Model T Ford taxi at the garage, now Brenchley Garage. The taxi was the property of the late Theo Gorringe, garage proprietor, who sold it to Percy Newington in April 1931.

A cottage opposite Petteridge lane remains almost untouched apart from the alterations to the windows and the addition of the oriole window above the door.

Above A View of William Hodges' home across Market Heath.
Below: Coal delivery at Market Heath.

JUGLANS HOUSE (THE WALNUT TREE), SWINGLE SWANGLE COTTAGES AND THE NEW CHAPEL ON THE BRENCHLEY ROAD

William Hodges' photograph of the Walnut Tree Public House (now Juglans House, Juglan being the botanical name for walnut tree) shows a large porch which was later demolished. The building continued to be used as a pub until the late 1990's, when it was converted to residential use. The present owners, dismayed at the condition of the bricks when the rendering to the front of the house was removed, launched into a nine month project to turn every brick around. Nicholas West painstakingly cut out and turned the bricks, 80% of which were re-usable. When the scaffolding was finally removed, the house was revealed in all its restored Georgian glory.

'Swingle Swangle Cottages', situated next to the old Walnut Tree Pub, were associated with Parish Relief. These were alms houses in the mid-nineteenth century until those who would have occupied them were transferred to the Pembury Institution, now Pembury Hospital. The 'Baptist Chapel', opposite 'Swingle Swangle Cottages', was built in 1891. Before that time meetings were held in a small cottage near to the site. The congregation grew, and apparently as many as ninety people were sometimes packed into "a moderate sized room" ('Light & Truth' 1891). The necessity for a new building became essential and the Old Baptist Union General Building Society came to the rescue. The opening services and celebrations lasted for three days and donations and collections over this period amounted to £13. 9s. 10½d (just under £13.50).

MARLE PLACE HOUSE AND GARDENS

The house is Jacobean and the date 1619 can be seen on the porch. Alterations, refurbishment and additions have gone on over the years, with the rear addition dated 1858. The beautiful gardens which surround the house were first created in 1890 and there are many early features: a Victorian greenhouse and gazebo, a walled garden built in 1900 and an Edwardian rockery. The greenhouse can be seen in William Hodges' photographs.

In 1841 the property was owned and farmed by Ann Fuggle. The Fuggle family discovered a hop which is named after them. The Fuggle hop is long and full of pollen and is still in use today for stronger beers. Today the gardens and an artists' gallery and studio are open to the public from the spring through to the autumn.

Marl is a lime-rich mud, which contains 35-65% clay. The lime content proved invaluable for spreading on ground intended for lime-loving crops. The name indicates a valuable source of marl in the vicinity. Marl pits were dug all over the parish and Parish Records list a number of deaths due to accidents whilst digging marl.

A group of fields round the footpaths from the butcher's shop in Brenchley to Palmers Green, just over the first stile, shows a number of unnatural depressions. A well worn track, some feet lower than the field level, follows the field boundary. It is likely that it is a site where marl was dug. The names of the fields indicate that this would have been agricultural work done by the occupants of Brenchley Workhouse: 'Workhouse Pit Field'; 'Workhouse Pit Shaw'; 'Right Hand Workhouse Pit Field' and 'Workhouse Pit Wood'.

Above: The photograph shows Thomas Guest, farmer and hop grower, who lived at 'Chillmill Manor' in 1884.
Below: 'Chillmill Manor'at the present time.

CHILLMILL

The earliest mention of this name is in 1334-1335 in the Kent Lay Subsidy Roll for the Hundred on Brenchley when we read of Thomas and Simon de Cheldmelle. The house, as we know it now, dates from the late 16th or early 17th century, probably with an earlier core. There have been alterations and later additions to the rear over the years.

Around the late 16th century William Lombarde, Queen's Proctor to Elizabeth I and author of 'Perambulations of Kent', owned a lot of land in Brenchley, including 'Brattles', 'Chillmill' and 'Curtiss'. It appears that 'Brattles' and 'Chillmill' were part of a single land holding. William Lombarde was a friend of the Roberts family, also landowners in Brenchley. On his death Lombarde willed land to the Drapers' Company. In 1898 the Governors of Greenwich College, founded by Lombarde, sold the estate of 750 acres to Mr D'Arcy Wentworth Reeve, a Brenchley farmer.

For most of the Victorian era the Guest family were tenant farmers of the estate. Joseph Guest paid £50 per year, in 1835, to rent 'Chillmill'. The Hodges' photograph possibly shows Thomas Guest, farmer and hop grower, who lived here in 1884.

Today, like so many farms, the farm buildings, including the oast house and the 17th century barn, have all been converted into separate dwellings.

WHEELWRIGHTS COTTAGES, MILE OAK

'Wheelwrights Cottages' from the east, with residents old and new.

Above: 'Wheelwrights Cottages' when run as a Public House by Mr. and Mrs. Curd.
Below: Mr and Mrs John Lenton, who live there now.

MATFIELD CHURCH

In 1830 the railway came to Paddock Wood and there was a proposal that the line would go through Matfield (at the Wish). Matfield, a small hamlet built around Matfield House, began to develop as a residential village for London businessmen. The Reverend Richard Davies, who came to the Parish of Brenchley in 1845, started working for a new church to be built in Matfield. After his death, the Reverend Francis Storr continued with the project but it wasn't until 1874 that the decision was made to go ahead. One of Francis Storr's curates was his son, Charles, who became the first vicar of the new church.

Subscriptions came in from near and far and plans were drawn up by Francis's nephew, Basil Champneys. Land just outside the village, near Cork's Pond, was donated and, in 1876, St. Luke's Church was finally built, costing £1,400. The Bishop of Dover consecrated the church on Friday, 13th October.

Matfield now thrived as a separate ecclesiastical parish from Brenchley. Charles and his wife Katherine moved, with their family, to Matfield. They later built a house in Sophurst Lane where they ran Matfield Grange School. There were Bible classes, Mothers' Meetings, Sunday School and trips to the seaside. A meeting hall was built near the village green. This was only demolished recently when the new Matfield Village Hall was built, and two houses were built on the actual site of the old hall (now known as 'Parish Hall Place'). A strong church-going village community was established.

After the first World War, 'Cork's Pond' was drained to make a suitable site for the new war memorial. The memorial, listing 24 names of men from Matfield who had died, was unveiled on 20th November 1920 by Lt. Col. H.H. Spender Clay. The Reverend Charles Storr read a passage from Corinthians I, chapter 15, "O God, our help in ages past" was sung and the Last Post was sounded, followed by a silence.

Above: The Matfield War Memorial.
Below: The interior of St. Luke's .

IN
LOVING MEMORY OF
THERESA GEORGINA SASSOON
WHO DIED 11TH JULY 1947
AGED 90 YEARS
MOTHER OF
MICHAEL SIEGFRIED AND
HAMO

SIEGFRIED SASSOON

The celebrated 1st World War poet Siegfried Sassoon was born at Weirleigh on Gedges Hill, Matfield, in 1886. In his books 'Memoirs of a Fox-Hunting Man' and 'The Old Century' he describes growing up in the Parish: the people he knew playing cricket in Brenchley, the watercress well at Moatlands and roaming the countryside. His mother, Theresa, was buried in Matfield churchyard and her gravestone and inscription are shown here.

Below: 'Cork's Pond' before it was drained to make way for the War Memorial.

MATFIELD HOUSE

This beautiful house, along with All Saints' Church, Brenchley, are the only Grade I Listed buildings in the Parish.

It was built in 1728 for Thomas Marchant, the penniless second son of a yeoman farmer from Burrs Hill, using his wife's money. He had married an 18-year-old orphaned heiress from Pattyndenne Manor near Marden, called Mary Bold. They eloped and were married in Fleet prison.

There are similarities between Matfield House and Finchcocks in Goudhurst and both buildings are believed to have been built by the same master builder, a man called Hodgkins. It is thought that the design for Finchcocks was obtained from the fashionable architect, Thomas Archer, well known for his work at Cliveden. The clock tower was added later, in 1736.

Two lead water pipes on either side of the front door are decorated with Thomas's and Mary's initials and the date 1728. There is also an heraldic decoration and the head of a woman, which could be that of Mary.

Mary did not have any children and it was rumoured that Thomas treated her very badly, keeping her locked in the attic. She died in 1751, at the age of 41, and Thomas married his housekeeper, Eleanor Taylor, who gave him two children: a daughter, Mary, and a son, Bold. On Thomas's death, aged 66, Bold took over the estate and ran it with great success, increasing the family fortune. Mary, Thomas and their children are buried in Brenchley churchyard and their railed grave can be seen to the right of the main path. Two brothers of Thomas, William and Nicholas, died in 1778 and 1779. Their tombstones in Brenchley churchyard tell us that they died of a "mortification of the foot".

The house stayed in the Marchant family until 1953. In the 1880s Walter Marchant lost a lot of money and was forced to sell some of the houses on the estate. In the 1920's it was let to E.W. Hubbard (see 'Matfield Brigade') and in 1950 Matfield Green was given to the Parish Council for the benefit of the village. In 1953 Walter Marchant sold Matfield House to Mr. Moore, who sold it to Sir William Garthwaite in 1960.

Left: Firemen in 1933
Standing: 3rd Officer F Giles.
Seated: left, Chief Officer Mr E Hubbard; right, 2nd Officer E Dodson.
The cups displayed are: left, The Deluge Cup; centre, Owles Cup and right, Wacher Trophy.
Below: The Matfield Fire Brigade on parade at Matfield House

Left: Crew Manager Johnston; Firemen Edwards, Tompsett; Watchmanager Underdown; Firemen Downes, Taylor, Norman; Crew Manager Gale; Trainee Sayers.

EARLY DAYS OF THE MATFIELD FIRE BRIGADE

Mr. E.W. Hubbard trained as an engineer with Mather & Platt of Manchester and before and during the early years of World War I he was engaged in their branch in Shanghai. The fire risk of the closely packed wooden houses in parts of Shanghai was considerable and Mr. Hubbard joined many of his colleagues in volunteering to help support the permanent staff of the fire brigade. He became a member of No. 4 Deluge Company, gaining much experience of fire and flood.

On moving to Matfield House in 1928 he invited the fire authority, then in Tunbridge Wells, to demonstrate the service available to Matfield. At a pre-arranged time, the brigade set out with their steam pump, pulled by a small agricultural tractor. When they arrived they pumped convincingly from the pond, throwing two jets right over Matfield House, but the time taken to cover the six miles convinced Mr. Hubbard that cover was inadequate to prevent tragedy, should life become involved.

He started a brigade in Matfield as the Tunbridge Wells Steam Fire Brigade ceased functioning. Subscriptions were raised and equipment collected. A hand-cart, a few reels of hose and second-hand uniforms were a good start. There were no pumps so hydrants were the only means of getting water to any fires. The first fire station was part of the cottages in front of Matfield House.

Luckily, the first fire alarm was very close at the Laundry on the other side of the pond. The firemen were called by two rockets fired from the Courtyard in Matfield House and by firemen running to each other's homes. The alarm was given at 2.24 a.m.; the firemen had assembled four minutes later, by which time the roof was ablaze. By 2.45 a.m. the fire had been extinguished. The delighted owner of the laundry, Mr Owles, presented a cup to the brigade, and Mr. Hubbard's former colleagues, still in Shanghai, sent the 'Deluge Cup', designed and made locally.

The History Society archive has a wonderful photograph album full of photographs of early fire-fighting machines, fire damage and the local men who fought the flames. At 2 a.m. on 15th August 1939 the fire station itself caught light, but the fire engine and equipment was saved just before the roof fell in. Today it is a great comfort to residents of Matfield and Brenchley to see our smart fire station with its modern equipment so close at hand.

THE STAR

THE STAR INN AND MATFIELD'S BUTCHER'S SHOP

Parts of this public house in the centre of Matfield date back to the late 1500s, with additions, including the front facing the road being added in the late 18th or early 19th century. It was originally built as a dairy farm and an historical guide in the pub states that it was bought by Robert Arnolde, brewer and ale seller of Brenchley, in 1637 and was registered as an inn in 1705. This guide also tells us that the thatch was replaced with tile in 1790.

Joseph Wenham was the Innkeeper between 1851 and 1861 and the corner where the butcher's shop stands was known as 'Wenham's Corner'. In 1871 his son Joseph was at the Star but he was also described as a butcher in the census. The census of 1881 describes John Smith, who was then in residence, as 'Victualler and Butcher'.

The present butcher's shop was built in the early 1870s on the site of a huge chestnut tree. As you can see from the old photograph the shop was designed to hang meat outside and in the windows. The windows were removable and there were thick marble slabs around the inside for cutting on and selling over. Nowadays of course customers go into the shop and the marble slabs have been removed. The shop has been a butchers to the present day. The present owners, Mark and Sons have run it since 1977.

Sheep grazing on Matfield Green.

Above: Matfield Butchers, pre 1914, run by Alf Chacksfield, at a time when health and safety precaution were much more relaxed than they are nowadays. Below: Helen Edmeads, Malcolm Wilson, Michael Hodd and Mark Edmeads.

Above: 'Masters' and the 'Old Laundry' seen across Matfield Pond taken by Hodges circa 1880. At this time 'The Cottage' had a thatched roof.

THE OLD LAUNDRY BESIDE THE DRYING GREEN, MATFIELD

Miss Violet Owles died in April 1982 and this brought her family involvement in the Matfield laundry to an end. By an Agreement dated September 1917 Walter Marchant, Esquire, (Landlord) agreed to "let to Mr. John James Owles (Tenant) all that Cottage, Garden and Premises, formerly known as Benge's situate in Matfield, lately in the occupation of Mrs. A.E. Rich, for use as a Laundry. Together with the right of hanging out clothes to dry on that part of Matfield Green situate east of the main road from Brenchley to Tunbridge Wells".

For over 200 years the laundry had flourished, together with the unusual right to hang out clothes to dry on what is still known as the 'Drying Green'. When Miss Owles's parents died she continued the business with the help of her 91 year old aunt, Mrs. Grace Morris, and two assistants. Satisfied customers had been sending their laundry for nearly 50 years and others who moved away still continued to send their washing; every week parcels came all the way from London.

First, the washing was put into a wooden washing machine or washed by hand. It was then rinsed and hung out on the drying green, just as it always had been for over two centuries. If it rained, the washing was dried round a large old stove. The ironing was done with heavy hand irons which were heated round an octagonal stove.

The 'Old Laundry' undergoing extensive refurbishment in the 1960s.

Workers in the Laundry: Miss Owles is attending to the irons – upper left and below to the mangle.

Every article was patiently and carefully ironed, fresh irons being taken from the hot stove every few minutes. Miss Owles was an expert with a hand made goffering iron which she used for christening robes. She would spend hours on them, sometimes ironing robes over a hundred years old. Table linen and napkins were given special attention; they were put through a massive 150 year old wooden box mangle, while damp, so that they were just ready for ironing. The washing wound round rollers and was pressed by a wooden box filled with rocks. The local washing was collected on a Monday morning and was always returned the following Saturday.

The box mangle (150 years old) is now in the Tunbridge Wells Museum. Several goffering irons and an ordinary flat iron on a trivet have been given to the History Society for safe keeping.

On 22nd October 1929 at 2.45 a.m. the newly formed Matfield Fire Brigade was called to its first fire at the old Laundry. This was caused by a faulty flue from the copper, which set fire to a wooden lath and plaster wall and to the roof. The fire was extinguished in 15 minutes. In attendance was the Chief Officer and the Second Officer and firemen Fuller, Giles, Carter, A. Newbold, sub-officers Chacksfield, Newbold and Dobbs. Mr. Owles was later to present a cup to the Brigade in grateful thanks, called the 'Owles Cup'.

On 22nd April 1942 the Laundry passed out of the hands of the Marchant family and in the late 60s Miss Owles semi-retired.

Matfield centre with the butcher's shop and the 'Star'.

MATFIELD GREEN

'Hatherleigh', the Green, Matfield. The house was rented by the Sassoon family from the married daughter of a former vicar of Matfield, while they were waiting to move into their house, 'Weirleigh', on Gedge's Hill .

'Matfield Court', Matfield Green: Henry Storr built Matfield Court and probably gave the adjacent land for the building of the first village hall.

View across Matfield green – with traffic!

THE FORGE, FORGE COTTAGE,THE WHITE HOUSE, MATFIELD

Forge Cottage, the central part of this building on Matfield Green, is the oldest part and probably dates from the late 17th century. Although the 'White House' shares the same deep mansard roof, it was added around the early 18th century. 'The Forge' was added at the end of the 18th century and we can probably assume that there has been a forge in operation there from this time until well into the 20th century. Some of the windows of 'Forge Cottage' retain some fine blacksmith-made window furniture with spring catches decorated with iron scrolls.

In 1912 the forge was taken over by a Mr. Oliver Firrell, whose family had been blacksmiths for 300 years. He had started work at thirteen in his father's forge in Brede and took his first job away from home, four years later, in Ticehurst. At weekends he would walk the sixteen miles to go home. Over the years he worked in Bethersden, Pluckley and Halstead and eventually had his own forge back in Brede until he retired to Burwash. But somehow he didn't take to retirement, which is when he bought the Matfield forge and eventually became known as 'Britain's Oldest Working Blacksmith'. We have in the archives newspaper cuttings from 1936, 1937 and from 1938 when he reached the age of ninety and was still working. He is reported as saying that he remembered the troops coming home from the Crimean war; and he had conversed on several occasions, while in Burwash, with Rudyard Kipling. He enjoyed showing how, at this great age, he could hold his smithy shovel between his first and second fingers and balance a 7lb. iron bar on the end! (There are photographs to show him doing this!)

Mr. Oliver Firrell

Right: Mr Thomas Homewood

STANDINGS CROSS, MATFIELD AND MR. HOMEWOOD

This public house on the main crossroads in Matfield was built around 1700. It is not clear if it has always been an ale-house, and there was probably a bakery to the rear at some time.

In the early part of the 20th century the pub was owned by Mr. Thomas Homewood, who also acted as village carrier, as his father had before him. Mr. Homewood, when younger, travelled as far as Maidstone, but in his later years he travelled between Matfield and Paddock Wood, going up and down the long and steep Gedges Hill. This would have taken him past Weirleigh, the house in which Siegfried Sassoon, the World War I poet, grew up.

In his book 'Memoirs of a Fox-Hunting Man' Siegfried Sassoon describes his meeting with 'Mr. John Homeward'. He writes, "I seldom spoke to anyone while I was out for my walks, but now and again I would meet John Homeward, the carrier, on his way back from the county town, where he went three days a week. Homeward had been making his foot-pace journeys with his hooded van and nodding horse ever since I could remember ……. All the year round, whether there was snow on the ground or blossom on the fruit trees, the carrier's van crawled across the valley with its cargo of utilities but Homeward was always alone with his horse for he never took passengers. His burly figure and kindly bearded face must have gone up and down that hill about five thousand times before he retired to prosper with a small public house".

Today the Standings Cross pub is called 'Morello' and continues to bestow food, drink and hospitality under the care of Brian Hodge.

THE FRIARS ESTATE, MATFIELD

Friars Farm appears to have originally consisted of 177 acres owned by Edward A. Dimmock, who employed seven labourers and three boys. In 1934 the estate consisted of the main house and four farm cottages. At that time it was purchased by Lady Bennett who, after extensive alterations, moved in with her entire staff from Speldhurst. During the 1939-45 war a detachment of the Canadian Army, en-route for the Dieppe landings, encamped in the field behind the oast. During their brief stay they demolished the entrance gate with one of their tanks. The estate was sold to a developer in 1968.

More of Hodges' portraits. Right: A gardener posed against a tree beside a pile of stakes he has cut. Below: A boy on a donkey.

KINGSMEAD, MATFIELD

No house is listed on the 1841 to 1861 census and, as it appears on the 1871 Ordnance Survey, 'Kingsmead' was probably built sometime between 1861 and 1871. The house was originally called 'Prospect House' and we know that a sixty five year old widower, Edward Moss Dimmock, lived there. He is described as a 'solicitor and landowner' and he had three servants, a gardener and a coachman.

In the 1881 census, the house is called 'Kings Mead' and Osborne Delano Osborne, a retired captain of the 55th Regiment, lived there with his wife, son, cousin and servants.

Above: Packing Red Cross parcels for the forces during the Second World war at Friars. Left to Right: Vera Potts, Kathleen Elles, Virginia Hubbard, Lady Bennett, Joan Rankin, Stephanie Bland.

London A21
Sevenoaks
Tunbridge Wells
MONSOON SPICE
Tel: 01892 822277

THE BLUE BOYS INN

In the village archive we have a copy of a letter, dated 31st October 1899, signed by 'L.E. Maude' of Horsmonden. It says: "The late Mr. Multon Lombarde told me that he had always heard from his father and, I believe, his grandfather too, that George IV, when driving in his coach and four from Penshurst to Bedgebury, was compelled to stop some time at your house while two of his horses were shod, the road from Pembury Lower Green to Kippings Cross then being simple execrable".

The Inn was named the 'Blue Boys' from the colour of the caps and jackets of the postillions. It was during his Regency that this happened, so the livery would not be scarlet, the present Royal colour. It is believed that the old sign used to be two Blue Postillions shaking hands and holding aloft a glass of foaming ale in the other hand.

Recently the inn has become an Indian restaurant.

THE KINGS TOLL CLUMP

A very large clump of trees standing away in the fields off the A21 near the Blue Boys is known locally as the Kings Toll Clump. This outstanding landmark was owned by Tunbridge Wells Borough Council but was sold to a private purchaser in the 1990s. It was used during the 1939-45 war by the Royal Air Force pilots as a landmark when returning to Biggin Hill.

ACKNOWLEDGEMENTS

The Brenchley and Matfield Local History Society has been in existence for thirty eight years and during this time many people have contributed photographs, memories, newspaper cuttings, books, old maps and drawings, albums, old church magazines and old deeds and papers to the Society. Most of these people are now unknown, and as this book has only been made possible because of the amazing content of our Village Archive, these unknown people must be acknowledged.

Of course many people are known: Ann Rabbitt who has done, and continues to do, endless research, and whose knowledge of the history of this parish is considerable; Sue Edwards, who was Chairman of the Society for many years, was instrumental in the huge task of beginning to collate the Archive into some sort of order, as well as doing her own research. Many people have contributed their knowledge of particular aspects of our history: Ann Williamson on Matfield House; Pom Gibbons on Siegfried Sassoon; Peter Lowe on The Workhouse; Brenchley Manor and Hatmill; Helen Edmeads on the Matfield butcher's shop; Malcolm Thomas on Wat Tyler; Dan and Anne Colman on Gate House Farm and Richard Dench on the Friars Estate. This acknowledgement would not be complete without mention of all the ladies of the Brenchley Afternoon Women's Institute. When they disbanded they donated their wonderful collection of albums, full of fascinating anecdotes and photographs of Brenchley village, to our Archive. William Hodges' glass plates are held at the County Archive in Maidstone. Other interesting old photographs in this book have been taken from the Village Archive. Neil Tester has let us use some of his old photos displayed in 'Terry's Butchers Shop'. The modern photographs in the book were all taken by Mike Daniels and Denise Barr, except for the black and white photograph on p.58 taken by Peter Stillwell. The postcard of the windmill and the interior of the Old Vicarage are reproduced with the kind permission of Ann Harris.

Grants from the Allen Grove Local History Fund of the Kent Archaeological Society and the Kent History Fund have helped our Society with the expense of publishing. A sub-committee of the History Society's committee, consisting of Denise Barr, Helen Brown, Roy Claydon, Michael Daniels and Pat Tottenham, has been instrumental in writing, producing and printing this book and Ann Williamson and Anne Colman have assisted with proof-reading. During this time Roy Claydon sadly died and we would like to thank the Claydon family for all their help in locating and retrieving from his computer all the work which Roy had completed. Since Roy's death Lynne Butler, who already does so much in our Parish, came to the rescue and has worked tirelessly on her computer, editing, helping and advising, to bring this finished book to print.

We have done our best to give credit and acknowledgement to all who have helped in the production of this book. If we have missed anyone out... sincere apologies.

Denise Barr
Chairman
Brenchley and Matfield Local History Society